PREVENTING WORKPLACE VIOLENCE
Positive Management Strategies

Marianne Minor

A Fifty-Minute™ Series Book

This Fifty-Minute™ book is designed to be "read with a pencil." It is an excellent workbook for self-study as well as classroom learning. All material is copyright-protected and cannot be duplicated without permission from the publisher. *Therefore, be sure to order a copy for every training participant by contacting:*

1-800-442-7477

Menlo Park, CA
www.crisplearning.com

PREVENTING WORKPLACE VIOLENCE
Positive Management Strategies

Marianne Minor

CREDITS
Managing Editor: **Kathleen Barcos**
Editor: **Carol Henry**
Typesetting: **ExecuStaff**
Cover Design: **Nicole Phillips**

© 1995 by Crisp Publications, Inc.
Printed in the United States of America by Von Hoffmann Graphics, Inc.

CrispLearning.com

03 04 05 10 9 8 7

Library of Congress Catalog Card Number 93-73145
Minor, Marianne
Preventing Workplace Violence
ISBN 1-56052-258-5

LEARNING OBJECTIVES FOR:

PREVENTING WORKPLACE VIOLENCE

The objectives for *Preventing Workplace Violence* are listed below. They have been developed to guide you, the reader, to the core issues covered in this book.

Objectives

- ❏ 1) To help explain reasons for violence in the workplace

- ❏ 2) To present violence prevention strategies

- ❏ 3) To present laws relevant to violence in the workplace

- ❏ 4) To show how to deal with violence crises.

Assessing Your Progress

In addition to the learning objectives, Crisp Learning has developed an **assessment** that covers the fundamental information presented in this book. A 25-item, multiple-choice and true-false questionnaire allows the reader to evaluate his or her comprehension of the subject matter. To buy the assessment and answer key, go to www.crisplearning.com and search on the book title, or call 1-800-442-7477.

Assessments should not be used in any employee selection process.

ABOUT THE AUTHOR

Marianne Minor is a licensed clinical social worker and management consultant. She has taught management and leadership programs internationally for Fortune 500 companies. She has also taught in graduate management programs at San Jose State University and the University of San Francisco.

She has designed and conducted numerous training programs for high-tech manufacturing and utility companies. Marianne has consulted with school districts on how to implement human resource systems and decentralized decision making. She specializes in team building and leadership programs.

She is president of her own consulting firm, Marianne Minor and Associates, in Silicon Valley, California.

The author may be contacted through Crisp Publications.

ABOUT THE SERIES

With over 200 titles in print, the acclaimed Crisp 50-Minute™ series presents self-paced learning at its easiest and best. These comprehensive self-study books for business or personal use are filled with exercises, activities, assessments, and case studies that capture your interest and increase your understanding.

Other Crisp products, based on the 50-Minute books, are available in a variety of learning style formats for both individual and group study, including audio, video, CD-ROM, and computer-based training.

DISCLAIMER

The author accepts no responsibility for any outcomes of any action based on recommendations in this book. Always rely on your own best judgment. Danger assessment and the management of potentially violent situations are not exact sciences, and often involve some degree of risk. The opinions expressed here are based on my own work, experience, and research in the field. In any case, try whatever seems right based upon your assessment of the situation at the time.

The material in this book is primarily applicable to North America and Western Europe. Most research in the area of social violence has been developed in these geographic/cultural areas. Different cultures may have unrecognized pre-violent syndromes, or culturally driven signs and behaviors different from those presented here.

CONTENTS

ACKNOWLEDGMENTS

Many people have dedicated their time and expertise to this book. I'd like to thank Miller Minor for his initial comprehensive research, and Lisa Hughes Drake for her creative editing and input.

In addition, a special thanks goes to Mary Reichlin, John O'Laughlin, Mike Zanoni, Elinor Sheldon and Jack Early, for sharing their expertise and personal experiences in this area.

Dedication
This book is dedicated to my husband, Gregory C. Paraskou, who provided me with the initial impetus to write a book on this subject. His continuous support and interest in my literary endeavors is inspiring.

About the Cover

The Chinese pictogram P'ing is the character for peace. It is symbolized by a shield balanced by a single tongue of fire on each side.

INTRODUCTION

What do all of the following situations have in common?

- Tragedy struck an airline in 1987 when a gunman opened fire in the plane's cabin. All 43 passengers died when the plane crashed and exploded on a hillside. The gunman was believed to be a disgruntled ex-employee, fired for petty theft and previously under investigation for various other crimes. A note to the man who had fired him—this man was also aboard the flight—was found at the crash site; it read, "I asked for some leniency . . . I got none and you'll get none."

- Also in 1987, seven employees of a defense contractor in California were killed and five others wounded, by a former employee who forced his way into a company building. He was armed with 100 pounds of weapons and ammunition. The killings came four years after the man had begun sending threatening letters to a coworker and making verbal threats against his bosses to other former coworkers.

- A bank in Maryland became the site of a murder-suicide when an employee returned from lunch and shot four others, only one of whom survived. The employee then turned the gun on himself. For two hours, people on other floors sat terrified behind barricaded doors, unsure of what was happening.

- Since 1983, 34 employees of the U.S. Postal Service have been murdered at work, many of them by ex-Postal employees seeking revenge for their termination or lack of promotion. As a result, the Postal Service has revamped its approach to employee violence. Applicants' employment histories and possible criminal records are being carefully researched and screened. Labor management panels and a 24-hour hotline for reporting threats have been established.

All of these situations are examples of the growing epidemic of workplace violence. Experts agree that in 99.9 percent of these kinds of situations, warning signs existed but were not seen or heard. This book examines why these signs are not recognized, and provides the latest information on how to prevent violence in the workplace from occurring. We will explore how prevalent the problem is, what the warning signs are, and aggravating factors that can make an already difficult employee turn violent.

INTRODUCTION (continued)

We will examine why managers, coworkers and entire organizations go into denial on this issue and fail to take simple steps toward prevention. These steps should include knowing the typical profile of a potentially violent employee, how to use a comprehensive screening process to weed these people out, and how to develop positive management strategies to prevent critical incidents.

In addition, this book describes how to coach and counsel and, when necessary, evaluate and terminate difficult employees. You will become familiar with intervention strategies to use during a critical incident, while protecting the safety of your employees and yourself. And you will examine recommended approaches for getting your company back on track after a critical incident occurs.

Also included is a collection of case studies for your analysis, with which you can practice your knowledge of the concepts presented in this book. Finally, there is a list of professional resources that you may need to complete your crisis management team.

SECTION

I

Understanding Violence in the Workplace

"It's never a normal person who snaps. It's always an abnormal person, often in a pressure situation. Generally, it's a sad tale of tragic proportions because the harm is so foreseeable."

—Parker Dietz, Forensic Psychiatrist

DEFINITION OF WORKPLACE VIOLENCE

There are various levels of workplace violence. It can begin as simple insubordination and threats and escalate to murder, suicide or even arson. Experts use the term *critical incident* to describe events that could potentially lead to violence. Critical incidents can include refusal to follow company policy, antagonism toward customers, verbal wishes to hurt coworkers and/or management, and actual threats of a sexual or violent nature. Though often ignored or minimized by coworkers and management, it is crucial that these critical incidents are seen as warning signs and dealt with immediately, with positive management strategies. These strategies are described in depth later in the book.

For the purpose of this book, workplace violence is defined as any situation that may:

- Increase in intensity and threaten the safety of any employee

- Have an impact on any employee's physical and/or psychological well-being

- Cause damage to company property

> **violence:** the abusive or unjust exercise of power: an outrage or wrong. Physical force exerted for the purpose of violating, damaging or abusing.
>
> —*Webster's Illustrated Encyclopedic Dictionary*

DEFINITION OF VIOLENCE IN THE WORKPLACE (continued)

Workplace violence can include any of the following events:

► **THREATS.** In Silicon Valley, California, officials of one company took seriously the threats of an employee about to be laid off. He claimed that he was going to kill 30 of his fellow employees. Police discovered a cache of weapons when they arrested the man: 12 revolvers, assorted rifles, semiautomatic pistols and ammunition.

► **WORK-RELATED CONFLICT.** In San Diego, after a "tough year" in 1991, one company laid off several low-performing employees. In keeping with the company's personal approach to helping former workers, outplacement services were provided on-site for those affected. One ex-employee, considered by former coworkers to be a loner and judgmental religious fanatic, arrived one day at the plant, set off two bombs, shot out the switchboard and killed two company executives.

► **PERSONAL CONFLICT.** In Canada, the husband of an employee arrived at the work site and, in a jealous rage, shot and killed one of his wife's coworkers.

► **TAKING OF HOSTAGES.** Angry over the loss of retirement benefits, the former employee of a telephone company returned to the work-place and took several hostages, also destroying almost $10 million in equipment.

► **ATTACK BY OUTSIDER.** Nearly impossible to prevent, these events have a painful aftermath that must be managed. Perhaps the most memorable incident of random workplace violence is the slaying of 21 people by a crazed gunman in a fast-food restaurant in San Ysidro, California.

Violence in the workplace can come in all shapes, sizes and severity. As the numbers of these incidents increase, experts have been able to study the patterns and factors correlated with the increase and to develop a typical profile of a potentially violent employee, as well as a potentially vulnerable organization. By examining how companies and managers deal with or deny this problem, we can explore what works and what doesn't, and develop guidelines for the future.

FACTS ABOUT WORKPLACE VIOLENCE

What do you know about violence in the workplace? Consider the following facts and statistics:

- The United States is the most violent nation in the western world. In 1993, there were 110,000 reported incidents of violence in U.S. workplaces, causing 750 deaths and costing employers $4.2 billion.

- Predicting workplace violence is often difficult. However, most violent employees give warning signs before demonstrating violence on the job. If a worker threatens violence, he or she needs to be taken seriously.

- Homicide in the workplace is the fastest growing form of murder; the rate has doubled in the past 10 years.

- Eighty percent of all work-related homicide victims have been male.

- A person who is emotionally upset at work is two-and-a-half times more likely to commit violence if he or she is using drugs or alcohol.

- A fascination with weapons is one warning sign in a potentially violent employee.

- Violence prevention can start in the initial employment interview.

- Of those who commit workplace murders, 40 percent then commit suicide.

- It is likely that a worker who is violated or murdered at work (or the worker's family) may sue the company for not having protected the worker.

- About 42 percent of women who die in the workplace are murdered.

- Past violence is the single best predictor of future violence.

- Most U.S. companies have no plan to deal with crises of violence in the workplace.

FACTORS LINKED WITH INCREASED WORKPLACE VIOLENCE

It's not by chance that workplace violence has escalated over the past few years. Frustrated workers may respond violently to a variety of stress-related factors, but experts believe three major components are correlated with the recent increase in violent incidents:

► **SOCIETAL FACTORS.** Violence is a prevalent element in the media today, leading to an implied approval of that violence. Weapons are increasingly available, and there is a growing fascination with weapons as tools of power. Many different societal factors have contributed to the breakdown of families and communities nationwide.

► **ECONOMIC FACTORS.** Today's eroding economic climate, with its smaller salaries and fewer benefits, is unkind. Even stable companies are victims of downsizing, re-engineering and increased use of subcontractors rather than full-time employees. There is often a lack of re-entry opportunities for laid-off employees.

► **MANAGEMENT-RELATED FACTORS.** When firms employ outdated, impersonal methods to deal with employee complaints, disillusionment and a lack of trust toward management may develop. Wrongful discharge cases can stretch over years, allowing anger to build.

While these outside factors might contribute to someone committing a violent act, violent feelings usually have deeper roots within a person's psyche. Understanding the characteristics of violence-prone people is one of the keys to identifying individuals who might threaten or commit violence in the workplace.

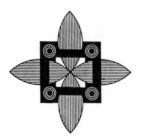 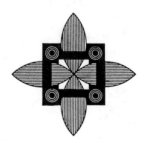

IDENTIFYING POTENTIALLY VIOLENT EMPLOYEES

> Although accurate predictions of violence are difficult to make, the best indicator of future behavior is past behavior. Indeed, the best predictor of future violence is a history of violence.

In the recent film *Falling Down*, Michael Douglas plays a man who, overwhelmed by the seeming unfairness of society, goes on a rampage of destruction. Experts agree that, unlike the screen character, people do not generally "snap." Violent people often give out many clues—even progressively serious clues—that they might violently act out their frustration.

The tragedy of workplace violence occurs when these clues are not recognized, or are not revealed to the next level of management. In this section you will find some tools to help you identify and evaluate indications of possible violent tendencies in workers, and circumstances that may contribute to the development of those tendencies.

DO ANY OF YOUR EMPLOYEES FIT THE FOLLOWING PROFILE?

PROFILE OF A POTENTIALLY VIOLENT EMPLOYEE

Experts agree that certain personality traits and mind-sets are common to violent employees. Be aware of the following traits in your employees.

- Has low tolerance for frustration

- Changes jobs frequently

- Is a marginal performer

- Is frequently angry

- Doesn't accept responsibility

- Blames others for mistakes and difficulties

- Lacks control of impulses

- Is defensive when criticized

- Abuses drugs and/or alcohol

- Is suspicious of others' motives

- Has entitlement mentality

- Is socially isolated; has few friends or family

- Has fantasies of retaliation; holds grudges

- Has history of negative inter-personal relationships

- Exhibits pattern of family violence or dysfunction

- Has low self-esteem

- Owns or has access to weapons

- Lacks empathy for others

- Is a Caucasian male in 30s or 40s

- Sees the company as a "family"

- Lacks adaptability to new work situations

Now that you know the traits of a potentially violent employee, let's examine some of the warning signs. These need to be recognized, acknowledged and addressed, for they are red flags that the employee may be losing control. The increase in intensity and frequency of certain disruptive behavior is an important indication that there may be rough times ahead.

ASSESSING WARNING SIGNS

If you are concerned about one of your employees, use the following check-list to assess what warning signs you may have noticed. Check the ones of which you are aware or that the employee has recently demonstrated.

☐ Frequent absenteeism

☐ Angry outbursts

☐ Sullen withdrawal

☐ Substance abuse

☐ Extreme disorganization

☐ Serious family problems

☐ Serious financial problems

☐ Ominous threats

☐ Intimidation of others

☐ Obsessions

☐ Romantic obsession/stalking

☐ History of violent behavior before or after current employment

☐ Obsessive involvement with job, with few outside interests

☐ Discussion of weapons or carrying of concealed weapon

☐ Increased frequency or intensity of above behaviors

___ **Total number of warning signs checked**

If you checked three or more of the above warning signs for a particular employee, you need to carefully monitor the situation. Use the positive management strategies outlined in Sections II through III to address the problem NOW! This may include enlisting support from employee assistance programs and getting some support for yourself, too, in assessment and intervention. Many managers who were interviewed for this book used their own human resource departments as well as outside professionals to help in managing a potentially violent employee.

Now that you are familiar with the warning signs of potential problems, let's look at the aggravating factors that may escalate the antagonistic behavior of a high-risk employee.

AGGRAVATING FACTORS

Certain circumstances can be catalysts for violent behavior in an already high-risk employee. If you are concerned about a specific employee who seems to fit the profile and has demonstrated several warning signs, continue your analysis by checking any of the following possible aggravating factors that apply.

Has the employee

☐ Received a bad performance review or disciplinary action

☐ Been part of a reduction in the workforce

☐ Been in conflict with his or her boss or a coworker

☐ Experienced a change in his or her personal or professional life

☐ Had family problems

☐ Experienced a loss of status, prestige, benefits, pay, or other negative impact to self-esteem

☐ Been terminated

☐ Had financial problems

☐ Shown evidence of alcohol or drug problems

☐ Had possible psychological issues due to mental illness

☐ Submitted a grievance that was ignored

— **Total number of aggravating factors checked**

> If you checked more than three factors in the above list, the employee may be under significant stress and may require professional assistance over and above your expertise as a manager. Follow the positive management strategies outlined in Section II to consider your alternatives.

IS YOUR ORGANIZATION PREPARED?

To rate your company at crisis management, check Yes or No for each of the items in this list.

Does your company

	Yes	No
Screen employees during the employment process for a history of violence?	☐	☐
Maintain security measures that provide appropriate protection for all employees?	☐	☐
Train managers on how to conduct reductions in force with sensitivity and compassion?	☐	☐
Teach managers to assess and attend to employees' emotional behavior?	☐	☐
Arrange outplacement services, including psychological assistance, for employees who are laid off?	☐	☐
Provide "survivor training" for those who are not laid off?	☐	☐
Provide "venting" systems, such as open-door policies, company advocates and grievance procedures?	☐	☐
Maintain employee assistance programs (voluntary) for all employees, and encourage employees to use the services during times of stress?	☐	☐
Have a comprehensive crisis management plan, including appropriate policies and procedures for dealing with violence?	☐	☐
During times of organizational change—restructuring, mergers, divestitures—provide workshops on the change process and how it will affect employees?	☐	☐

IS YOUR ORGANIZATION PREPARED?
(continued)

Count the number of Yes and No answers. If you checked more than three Nos, your company does not have sufficient preventive strategy in place and could be at risk for violent incidents. Use the recommendations in this book to develop resources and plans.

Now go back to the Nos you checked in this list. Decide what you think is most important for your company to focus on now. Take into account any recent changes that have occurred in your firm.

What resources do you have at your disposal to implement these actions?

_____

_____

_____

_____

What obstacles might prevent you from implementing them?

_____

_____

_____

_____

SECTION

II

Violence Prevention Strategies

*❝The longest journey is
the journey inward.❞*

—Dag Hammerskjold

PREVENTING CRITICAL INCIDENTS IS CRUCIAL

Managers are often overburdened with the daily demands of their jobs and spend every minute dealing with routine concerns and business-related crises. Though it may seem a poor use of time to plan for an event that might never happen, being caught unprepared at any stage of involvement with a violent or potentially violent person is simply not worth the gamble. Consider the possible impact to your business if a violent incident is not adequately handled. You may see

- Lower productivity

- Reduced profitability

- Poor morale

- Increased absenteeism

- Higher sick leave costs

- Faster personnel turnover

- Strained management-employee relationships

> **Remember:** Workplace violence affects not only victimized employees, but also coworkers, the family members of victims, and managers at all levels.

In this section you will have an opportunity to examine your own and your company's readiness to deal with workplace violence and its early symptoms.

BEING PREPARED CAN MAKE A DIFFERENCE

Certainly, a manager does not have control over all the variables that may motivate a violent employee to act out. These events can range from organizational changes such as layoffs and mergers, to emotional situations such as racial conflicts, domestic disputes and mental illness, to global problems such as a poor economy.

Violence rarely erupts, however, until after the employee has become convinced that no other remedies are available. This means that troubleshooting on your part—using positive management principles and strategies to deal with the employee's problems—*can* make a difference.

Although violent employee behavior cannot always be predicted, in some circumstances you can prevent it from occurring altogether.

> A recent survey published in *Fortune* magazine of the United States's top 1,000 industrial and top 500 service companies revealed that of those who responded, only 53 percent have a plan for communicating quickly and efficiently during times of crisis.

The Role of Managers

It is the role of the manager to set limits about appropriate behavior at work, to enforce standards and policies, and to deal with difficult employees in a positive way—*early on*—so that negative feelings do not fester. In many cases of workplace violence, the problems and warning signs were ignored or not directly handled. The situations continued and worsened, with employees building up resentment and carrying grudges. Effective crisis managers know how to use positive management strategies on the job to prevent critical incidents.

Mistakes Managers Make in Assessing Violence Issues

The first step in violence prevention is examining your own behavior and beliefs. Following are some mistakes to avoid in order to be better prepared to deal with critical incidents. Check those that you have either observed or directly experienced.

☐ You believe your company is immune from crisis.

☐ When an employee begins to behave in a bizarre fashion, you deny that there is a problem.

☐ You do not take threats seriously.

☐ You do not document threats.

☐ You do not use a comprehensive employee-selection process.

☐ Involved in your own work or absent from the workplace, you do not notice warning signs of trouble.

☐ You discount or ignore other employees' complaints about the belligerent behavior or escalating hostility of another employee.

☐ You have not provided appropriate training and coaching for employees to learn and get satisfaction from doing their jobs.

☐ You have not provided ongoing feedback to employees, instead unloading all bad news during appraisal sessions.

☐ You have not followed appropriate early disciplinary procedures, or have failed to terminate an employee who is unable or unwilling to perform job duties.

☐ The company is lax in enforcing its sexual harassment policies.

Seriously review any item with a checkmark. Your goal with this exercise is to eliminate all checkmarks. It is normal to hope that a problem will resolve itself or just go away. But this kind of faulty thinking can endanger you and others. In general, if left alone, trouble in the workplace tends to worsen over time, rather than improve.

ARE YOU AN EFFECTIVE CRISIS MANAGER?

Use the following 20 behaviors to check your knowledge of preventing violence in the workplace. Read on to get more information about the items checked in the "will use" column.

	Already using	Will use
1. Implement a comprehensive selection process to screen out potentially violent employees as much as possible.	☐	☐
2. Set realistic workloads, work schedules and work pace for all employees. Allow employees some "down time" after the completion of strenuous assignments.	☐	☐
3. Provide clearly defined goals, roles and procedures for working together.	☐	☐
4. Design jobs so they provide challenge, stimulation and a sense of accomplishment for employees.	☐	☐
5. Give workers an opportunity to have input into decisions that affect them.	☐	☐
6. When appropriate, allow employees some discretion in how they perform their job duties.	☐	☐
7. Be clear about your expectations and standards as manager. Define what is acceptable workplace behavior.	☐	☐
8. Provide opportunities for employees' professional growth (training, mentoring, etc.).	☐	☐
9. Provide support during stressful times—as when mergers, acquisitions, layoffs, or changes in leadership occur.	☐	☐
10. Arrange employee assistance programs (EAPs) to help employees handle stress, change and personal problems that may affect job performance.	☐	☐
11. Coach employees about performance issues *before* they become serious problems. Provide regular, high-quality feedback about performance, to avoid "surprises" during formal appraisals, disciplinary actions and terminations.	☐	☐

	Already using	Will use

12. Closely supervise difficult employees and help them remove barriers to job performance. Encourage them to correct substandard performance, and if they don't improve, follow a disciplinary action procedure. (There is one described later in this book.) Terminate employees who cannot perform their jobs to expectations. ☐ ☐

13. Counsel employees about organizational changes. ☐ ☐

14. Provide grievance policies and procedures for employees who feel they have been treated unfairly. Give employees access to an advocate who will allow them to vent frustrations and help them work through channels to solve problems. ☐ ☐

15. Provide physical security in the workplace. ☐ ☐

16. Invest in safety awareness training for all employees. ☐ ☐

17. When downsizing, exit interviews should be conducted by someone other than the person who delivered the bad news, so that employees can vent feelings of anger and helplessness. Working through their feelings allows them to move on to acceptance of their situation. ☐ ☐

18. Create a comprehensive crisis management plan that involves all levels of the organization, as well as community resources. Form a crisis management team that will develop policies and procedures for handling crises during middle and late stages. ☐ ☐

19. Develop a communication network to keep employees informed about organizational changes that may affect them. ☐ ☐

20. Provide training programs for management on recognizing warning signs, learning the profile of a potentially violent employee, and what to do before, during and after a critical incident. ☐ ☐

THE ELEMENTS OF PREVENTION

Many companies are unprepared to handle workplace violence, operating under the myth of "it could never happen here." Experts agree that companies that are proactive in this area are able to protect lives, prevent damage to company property, and save millions of dollars by avoiding lawsuits and lost productivity.

The Nine Elements

✔ Assemble a Crisis Management Team

✔ Mobilize Professional Advisors

✔ Create a Crisis Management Plan

✔ Establish a Violence-Protection Policy

✔ Know Your Employment Laws

✔ Use Proper Employee-Selection Techniques

✔ Recognize Signs of Trouble

✔ Provide Coaching or Counseling

✔ Take Disciplinary Action

✔ ASSEMBLE A CRISIS MANAGEMENT TEAM

The crisis management team's mission is to create a comprehensive management plan and to prevent and monitor critical incidents over time.

Does your company have a crisis management team? Experts agree that the team should be composed of representatives from the following groups:

- *Senior Management,* to determine specific responsibilities during a crisis. They should designate a spokesperson, as well as a senior manager to be responsible for organizing a team response to the crisis.

- *Security Personnel,* to provide input on current security measures to be used for effective prevention and intervention.

- *Medical Personnel,* for expertise on assessment of substance abuse and/ or medical conditions that could lead to disruptive behaviors.

- *Legal Advisors* with knowledge about policies, procedures and steps to take to protect employees. They can also reduce the potential liability by informing and training managers on current employment laws.

- *Human Resources Managers,* depending on their training and experience, to provide input about assessment, organizational change and its effects, and to recommend policies and procedures for a safe workplace.

- *Employee Assistance Professionals,* to help identify high-risk employees, provide counseling to employees and families and to conduct group support sessions after major organizational change and violent events. They can also provide training on stress reduction, substance abuse and identification of mental illness.

- *Public Relations Experts* with knowledge of how to handle the press during a crisis, so as not to damage the company's image.

- *Community Representatives,* such as local law officers and fire fighters, to provide expertise and plan for immediate assistance in a violent situation.

- *Investigators* to do background checks on employees who have made threats, and determine their criminal history and current living situation. They can also provide protection to a threatened employee.

- *Assessment Experts,* to conduct a threat assessment by examining an employee's history and patterns of behavior, and to make recommendations for protecting employees and company property.

These groups of professionals may already exist in your organization, or you may have to subcontract with outside resources (see Resource Appendix).

ASSEMBLE A CRISIS MANAGEMENT TEAM (continued)

In the chart below, draw lines to the groups that already exist in your organization:

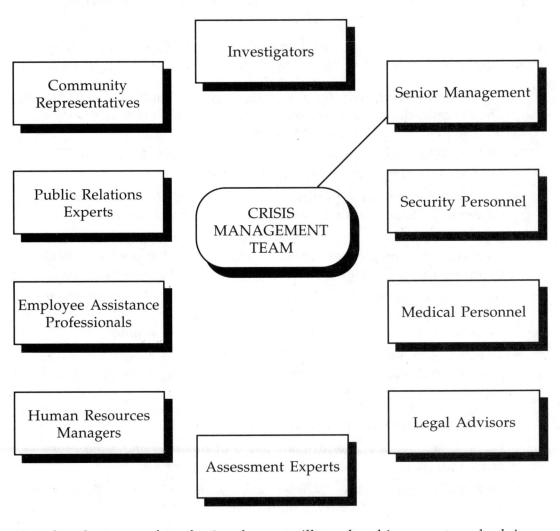

Now list the types of professionals you will need to hire as external advisors or consultants:

- _____
- _____
- _____
- _____

YOUR CRISIS MANAGEMENT TEAM

Who will be on *your* crisis management team? List the names of specific professionals and/or organizations in whom you have confidence.

Senior Management: _____

_____

_____

Security: _____

_____

_____

Medical: _____

_____

_____

Legal Advisors: _____

_____

_____

Human Resources: _____

_____

_____

Employee Assistance: _____

_____

_____

Public Relations: _____

_____

_____

CRISIS MANAGEMENT TEAM (continued)

Community Respresntatives: _____

_____

_____

Investigators: _____

_____

_____

Assessment Experts: _____

_____

_____

✔ MOBILIZE PROFESSIONAL ADVISORS

Support services can be a crucial part of the intervention process. Support services include employee assistance programs, mental health counseling, outplacement services and "survivor training" (offered to those who remain in the workplace but are grieving).

Acquiring Professional Help

Outside assistance is invaluable when you need employee counseling, legal advice and other trauma-related services. Trained professionals can provide up-to-date advice on how to prevent lawsuits and can offer significant emotional support for employees who need it. Investigate various services *before* you need to use them. There are three primary categories to look at:

► **Employee Assistance Programs**

► **Assessment Professionals**

► **Legal Assistance**

Employee Assistance Programs

Employee assistance programs (EAPs) can help you with both prevention and handling of critical incidents. They will

- Help identify high-risk employees or family members

- Provide counseling for employees

- Conduct group support sessions

- Provide consultation during crisis management planning

- Conduct training programs on how to deal with critical incidents in the workplace as well as normal reactions to violence

- Assess the needs of both individuals and organizations in preventing and dealing with violence

MOBILIZE PROFESSIONAL ADVISORS (continued)

Assessment Professionals

Assessment experts are invaluable when you need a trained eye to help estimate a situation or an individual. These services include

- Threat assessments, by evaluating the root cause of the problem. (For example, are an employee's violent tendencies due to mental illness or long-repressed anger?)

- Recommendations about how to protect employees and company property

- Analysis of a person's potential for violence

- Recommendations for legal and disciplinary actions

Legal Assistance

Your legal responsibilities are likely to be complex and will vary widely based on the situation. Legal advisors can

- Assist your crisis management team during the planning stages

- Advise you on policies, procedures and steps to take during disciplinary or termination proceedings, as well as give protection advice

- Reduce your potential liability by educating management on current employment and other pertinent legal information

✔ CREATE A CRISIS MANAGEMENT PLAN

Once you've assembled your team, you'll need to have an agenda for creating your company's crisis management plan. The plan created by your team should be comprehensive and should have at least these eight elements:

► **Policy:** Your company's stance on handling critical incidents and documenting crises. (A sample policy statement is provided later in this section.)

► **Procedures:** How crises will be handled, with specific actions clearly outlined.

► **Role Definitions:** Assignments of who does what, when and where in a crisis.

► **Communication Plan:** How to notify employees and families of a crisis situation.

► **Spokesperson:** The person who will deal with the media.

► **Public Relations Plan:** Guidelines on what information will be disclosed and to whom.

► **Professional Contacts:** Internal and/or external resources and support; for example, immediate counseling for traumatized employees.

► **Logistics Plan:** How your company will handle physical issues such as restoring damaged equipment, providing security for employees sent home, and activating a backup communication system.

Once Human Resources has reviewed each element of the plan, this completed plan should be written out and distributed to each member of the crisis management team. Review the plan occasionally and be certain that each member of the team knows his or her responsibilities.

✔ ESTABLISH A VIOLENCE-PREVENTION POLICY

The policy your company adopts to address violence and threats of violence should be strong and unambiguous, describing the firm's intent to resolve acts of violence in the workplace. Here is a sample:

Sample Policy

_____ Company maintains the policy that any violent acts or threats of the same, made by an employee against another person's life, health, well-being, family or property, are entirely unacceptable and cause for immediate dismissal. This policy holds for any threats made on Company property, at Company events or under other circumstances that may negatively affect the Company's ability to conduct business. Such acts or threats of violence, whether made directly or indirectly, by words, gestures or symbols, infringe upon the Company's right or obligation to provide a safe workplace for its employees.

An employee who believes that he or she has been the target of violence or threats of violence, or has witnessed or otherwise learned of violent conduct by another employee in the capacity described above, should contact Human Resources and his or her immediate manager immediately.

✔ KNOW YOUR EMPLOYMENT LAWS

Your company and its managers have important duties and legal obligations in violence prevention and worker protection. Make sure you have taken steps to comply with the following regulations and guidelines.

► The Federal Occupational Safety and Health Act (OSHA) requires employers in certain situations to take preventive measures in response to a threat by an employee against another company employee(s).

► Federal OSHA requires that an employer take steps to insure a safe and healthful workplace for its employees.

► An employer may be found negligent in its hiring of an employee where it has failed to investigate the references and prior work history of that employee, when the investigation would have revealed that employee's violent past behavior.

► An employee who is discharged because of accusations of violent tendencies can sue for wrongful discharge. The actual incidents of gross misconduct must be fully documented.

► After a full investigation has taken place that has shown potential for violence, an employer might be required to warn employees of the violent tendencies of a fellow employee. When the employer warns other employees of a fellow employee's violent tendencies and the employer's belief is mistaken, that employee may sue for defamation.

► In California (although not in all states), a therapist who believes his or her patient is a danger to another person has a duty to warn the identified intended victim of impending danger.

► A worker can be compensated by Worker's Compensation for any injuries suffered as a result of violence at his or her place of employment.

KNOW YOUR EMPLOYMENT LAWS
(continued)

► An employer may require a prospective employee to take a psychological examination only if the questions are relevant to job performance or there is another compelling reason, and the examination is required of all applicants.

► The Americans with Disabilities Act covers mental or emotional illness only if it amounts to a mental impairment.

A Word About Employment Laws

Employment laws vary significantly from state to state. If you have any questions about local, state or federal employment laws, you should seek qualified legal counsel.

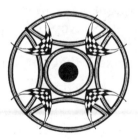

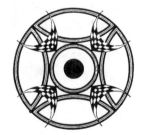
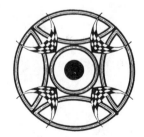

✔ USE PROPER EMPLOYEE-SELECTION TECHNIQUES

According to current employment laws, your organization can be considered negligent if a violent employee causes damage to other people and you did not institute proper screening when the employee was hired. To reduce your liability, you need to implement a comprehensive selection process.

Hiring Practices Assessment

Below are important measures for screening out potentially violent employees before they can do damage to your organization. Check Yes or No to indicate actions you currently take during the selection process.

	Yes	No
Conduct in-depth interviews with a variety of candidates.	☐	☐
Conduct pre-employment tests of specific job-related skills and abilities. Use psychological tests to screen applicants, if the tests are related to job performance. There are several useful tests on the market that help organizations determine applicants' dependability, drug avoidance and nonviolent tendencies (see the Resource Appendix for more information).	☐	☐
During the interview, to get at specific examples of successes and failures in past performance, ask behavioral questions focused on past performance rather than hypothetical future behavior.	☐	☐
To find out about possible discord with previous employers, ask questions such as "Tell me about the positive and negative aspects of your last employer."	☐	☐
Whenever possible, ask applicants to sign a legally reviewed consent form to obtain prior performance appraisals and to check with references. Applicants, however, *are not required* to grant your request.	☐	☐

USE PROPER EMPLOYEE-SELECTION TECHNIQUES (continued)

	Yes	No
Advise applicants that omissions, misrepresentation or falsification of information will result in rejection for employment or termination.	☐	☐
Check references and verify past employments.	☐	☐
Contact prior employers and seek specific information about the person's reliability, integrity and tendency for violence. (Be advised however, that for legal reasons former employers may not want to answer specific questions.)	☐	☐
Hire an outside firm to investigate applicants' signs of a troubled past, criminal *convictions*, substance abuse, driving violations, chronic bad debt, cycles of frequent employment change and gaps in the work history.	☐	☐

REMEMBER: EVERY "YES" BOX *SHOULD* HAVE BEEN CHECKED. EVEN ONE "NO" RESPONSE COULD PUT YOUR COMPANY AT RISK. YOU SHOULD NOT RETAIN EMPLOYEES AFTER A HISTORY OF VIOLENCE IS DISCOVERED.

✔ RECOGNIZE SIGNS OF TROUBLE

If an employee comes to you with a specific problem, great—your job as a manager has just been made easier. But how about those employees who never walk through your door, even though you say your "door is always open." You may have to rely on your skill to recognize signs of performance or attitude problems.*

Following are two lists of signs that can help you develop your managerial skills. Some will be obvious; others less so. You may have some signs of your own to add to the list.

SIGNS OF DECLINING PERFORMANCE	*SIGNS OF POOR ATTITUDE*
• Decreased productivity	• Takes little or no initiative
• Poor-quality work	• Withdrawn
• Missed due dates	• Disinterested
• Doing small tasks first	• Complains increasingly
• Avoiding tougher jobs	• Uncooperative
• Disorganized	• Blames failure on others
• Leaning on others for direction	• Defensive
• Away from desk for long periods	• Avoids contact with team members
• Upward delegation	• Lacks enthusiasm for job
• Absenteeism	• Irritability, depression
Add others:	Add others:
_____	_____
_____	_____
_____	_____

* For more information on this topic, order *Handling the Difficult Employee,* by Marty Brounstein, Menlo Park, CA: Crisp, 1993.

✔ PROVIDE COACHING OR COUNSELING

Coaching and counseling are two extremely valuable tools to which every manager has access. When practiced correctly, coaching and counseling can serve two primary functions: allowing you to offer constructive guidance to an employee who is having trouble performing his or her job duties; and redirecting any feelings of frustration and resentment—that could later lead to violence—into the improvement of job performance and self-esteem. The following section is designed to help you become a more effective coach and/or counselor, and to recognize when each role is needed.

Definitions

Coaching: A *directive* process by a manager to train and orient an employee to the realities of the workplace and help the employee remove barriers to optimum work performance.

Counseling: A *supportive* process by a manager to help an employee define and work through personal problems that affect job performance.

Counseling and coaching share many of the same skills. At times they may seem to overlap. When they do, remember the following two diagrams, which will help you differentiate the two processes:

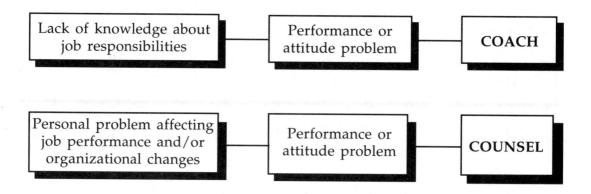

Work Situations That May Require Coaching

Check any that you have personally encountered:

☐   **1.** Teaching a new job skill

☐   **2.** Need to explain standards of the work unit

☐   **3.** Need to explain cultural norms and political realities of the organization

☐   **4.** Need to request simple corrections to performance

☐   **5.** Goals or business conditions change

☐   **6.** Being new to a group

☐   **7.** Employee faces new work experience

☐   **8.** Employee needs help setting priorities

☐   **9.** Follow-up to a training session

☐ **10.** Employee displays low or moderate performance

☐ **11.** Employee needs reinforcement for good performance

☐ **12.** Formal or informal performance reviews

☐ **13.** Employee needs preparation to meet future career goals

☐ **14.** Employee needs preparation for more challenging work assignment

☐ **15.** Employee needs to develop self-confidence

☐ **16.** Power or control battles are affecting team cohesiveness

Can you think of any other situations that may require coaching?

_____

_____

PROVIDE COACHING OR COUNSELING (continued)

Work Situations That May Require Counseling

Check any that you have personally encountered:

☐ **1.** Reorganizations

☐ **2.** Layoffs (requiring counseling for those who are laid off *and* those who are not)

☐ **3.** Demotions due to organizational changes

☐ **4.** Salary freezes; decreases in salary, status or responsibility

☐ **5.** Employee faced with no career opportunities inside the organization

☐ **6.** Employee unhappy with boss

☐ **7.** Employee unhappy with work assignment

☐ **8.** Employee has conflict with peer

☐ **9.** Employee feels stressed or burned out

☐ **10.** Employee feels insecure about job skills or performance

☐ **11.** Employee has been promoted and feels threatened

☐ **12.** Employee shares personal problem requiring support

☐ **13.** Employee has personal problems that are affecting performance of others

☐ **14.** Employee's performance problems persist

☐ **15.** Employee is experiencing failure

☐ **16.** Employee is disappointed in new job

Can you think of any other situations from your personal experience where counseling would have been effective?

_____

_____

Providing Effective Feedback

You should now know what coaching and counseling involve and when you should use each. Now you are ready to learn the most important skill to becoming an effective coach or counselor: how to provide honest feedback.

Whether you recognize it or not, you are constantly giving feedback. How you provide that feedback will often spell the difference between success or failure.

TYPES OF FEEDBACK

TYPE	DEFINITION	PURPOSE	IMPACT
SILENCE	• No response provided	• Maintain status quo	• Decreases confidence • Reduces performance • Produces paranoia • Creates surprises during performance appraisals
CRITICISM (negative)	• Identifies undesirable behaviors	• Stops undesirable behaviors	• Generates excuses/blaming • Decreases confidence • Leads to avoidance or escape • Can eliminate related behaviors • Hurts relationships
ADVICE	• Identifies results or behaviors desired and specifies how to incorporate them	• Shape or change behaviors or results to increase performance	• Improves confidence • Strengthens relationships • Increases performance
REINFORCEMENT (positive)	• Identifies results or behaviors that were desired, up to or exceeding standards	• Increase desired performance or results	• Boosts confidence • Heightens self-esteem • Increases performance • Enhances motivation

HOW TO GIVE EFFECTIVE FEEDBACK

1. Be *specific* when referring to behavior.

   Bad: "Henry, you are lazy and have a poor attitude toward your job."

   Good: "Henry, you have been 15 minutes late for the last three mornings. Please explain why."

2. **Consider your timing. Before the event, give feedback in the form of advice; immediately after the event, give positive feedback.**

   Bad: (criticism) "Sally, because you've done such a poor job in the past, I need to preview the speech you plan on giving next week."

   Good: (advice) "Sally, I'd like to review the content of your presentation before your speech next week so you can really do a good job in front of the group."

   Bad: (positive but not specific) "Sally, good speech last week. Keep up the good work!"

   Good: (positive) "Sally, you did an outstanding job in organizing your presentation for the meeting. The speech was well researched and logical."

3. **Consider the needs of the person receiving the feedback as well as your own. Ask yourself what he or she will get out of the information. Are you "dumping" or genuinely attempting to improve performance or the relationship?**

   Bad: "Sue, you always need help with the newsletter. It's not my responsibility. Don't you think it's about time you learned how to edit the newsletter?"

   Good: "Sue, I know how important it is to you to get the newsletter just right, and I recognize that you're under a lot of pressure right now. I will help you edit it this time, but I want you to take that editing class so you can handle it solo in the future."

4. **Focus on behavior the receiver can do something about.**

   Bad: "Sam, why are you so introverted that you don't like to talk to other people?"

   Good: "Sam, we would appreciate your keeping the team informed about the status of the project."

5. **Avoid labels and judgments by describing rather than evaluating behavior.**

   Bad: "Steve, you are very lazy about improving your skills and don't seem to care about your career here."

   Good: "Steve, I have given you five chances to attend training programs in the last year and you haven't enrolled yet. Is there a problem?"

6. **Define the impact on you, the unit, the team and the company.**

   Bad: "Sarah, can't you ever get your reports to me on time?"

   Good: "Sarah, when you don't get your report to me on time, I can't get my report to my boss on time. This slows up decisions about how resources are allocated to our team for the next month and how fast our company can service our customers."

7. **Use "I" statements as opposed to "You" statements to reduce defensiveness.**

   Bad: "Tim, you are so inconsiderate of other people when you leave your radio on."

   Good: "Tim, when you play your radio in the work area, I lose my concentration. Would you mind turning it off during regular work hours?"

HOW TO GIVE EFFECTIVE FEEDBACK (continued)

8. **Check to be sure your message has been clearly received.**

Bad: "Mary, I'm sure you got it all, huh?"

Good: "Mary, do you know what information I need you to record for all my phone messages? Can you explain it to me so I know you understand?"

9. **Give the feedback in calm, unemotional words, tone and body language.**

Bad: "Joe, you blew it again! Isn't it about time you improved your production with this machine!"

Good: "Joe, I think there might be some ways you can improve your production with this machine."

Feedback Pointers

► *Reinforcement* is the most effective form of feedback.

► *Criticism* is the most ineffective form of feedback.

► The difference between criticism and advice is a difference in *timing.* Most criticism can be given as advice.

► When feedback is mixed, the impact is diluted. The employee becomes confused and doesn't know what to do.

► Criticism overpowers all other feedback.

► Silence is not always "golden." It can be interpreted in a variety of ways.

POSITIVE FEEDBACK COMES IN MANY FORMS

Kinds of Reinforcement

In addition to one-on-one verbal reinforcement, employees may be motivated by other types of reinforcers. The best way to find out which are meaningful is to ask your employees directly and listen to their responses. Listen for values, interests and hobbies.

Here are 18 examples of reinforcements:

1. Being given control over job

2. Winning special projects

3. Having greater visibility among upper management

4. Receiving responsibility to a greater scope/depth

5. Having a choice about overtime

6. Having a choice about flex-time, schedule and/or vacations

7. Being offered the option to travel

8. Receiving flowers

9. Receiving money

10. Earning awards, such as a plaque

11. Receiving letters of praise

12. Having greater exposure among various parts of the organization

13. Receiving public praise

14. Receiving business cards or stationery

15. Having an improved office environment—new desk, window, office, etc.

16. Being given a dinner with spouse

17. Attending classes and conferences

18. Being asked to observe customer visits

What additional reinforcers might motivate your employees?

_____   _____

_____   _____

_____

PROVIDE COACHING OR COUNSELING (continued)

Guidelines for Successful Coaching

You are ready to begin a coaching session. You feel confident. Someone else will answer your phone. You are ready to listen. Your notes and pencil are in front of you. Your employee walks in, and you begin the session.

1. Put the employee at ease by being warm and friendly.

2. Define the reason for the discussion.

3. Express your concern about the area of performance that you feel needs to be improved.

4. Describe the performance problem or area that needs improvement and define its impact on you, the employee, the unit and the company.

5. Acknowledge and listen to the employee's feelings.

6. Seek the employee's opinion on ways to improve performance.

7. Ask open-ended questions to encourage employee's analysis and draw out specific suggestions.

8. Let the employee know that you respect his or her ability to solve problems and develop solutions.

9. Offer suggestions when appropriate, but build on the employee's ideas when possible.

10. Agree upon appropriate actions.

11. Promise to provide feedback on progress.

12. Schedule a follow-up meeting within ten days to ensure accountability and provide feedback on progress.

The session is over. You are relieved and pleased that it went so well. Congratulations!

Guidelines for Successful Counseling

You are ready to begin a counseling session. You feel confident. Someone else will answer your phone. You are ready to listen. Your notes and pencil are in front of you. Your employee walks in, and you begin the session.

1. Put the employee at ease by being warm and friendly and using positive body language, lots of eye contact and physically facing the person.

2. Define the reason for the discussion if you called the session, or encourage the employee to define its purpose.

3. Avoid judgmental words such as *should, must* or *ought.*

4. Ask open-ended questions about the employee's feelings and thoughts.

5. Paraphrase the content and emotional feelings of the employee's message.

6. Summarize key points at the end of the discussion, to clarify and seek understanding.

7. Encourage the employee to identify alternatives to solve the problem or resolve the issue.

8. Seek the employee's feelings and discuss the possible consequences of each of the alternatives.

9. Avoid expressing your views, but remain alert to provide information on company policies that may help the employee make a decision.

10. Demonstrate empathy for the employee, and show confidence in his or her ability to solve problems.

11. Offer support and/or resources when appropriate.

12. If the problem is beyond your scope, refer the employee to Human Resources and/or an employee assistance program.

13. Schedule a follow-up meeting with the employee to check on progress.

The employee leaves. You sigh, then pat yourself on the back. You've completed a successful counseling session! Congratulations!

NOW WHAT? WHEN COACHING AND COUNSELING FAIL

Occasionally, despite coaching or counseling sessions, an employee's performance may continue to deteriorate or remain below acceptable standards.

When this happens, you as manager must take responsibility for remedying the situation. Before determining the best choice, answer the questions next to each alternative below.

ALTERNATIVES	QUESTIONS TO ASK YOURSELF FIRST
1. *Restructure existing job*	• Does the employee possess enough strength in key areas of the restructured job? • Can tasks be eliminated or delegated where employee's performance is below standard?
2. *Transfer employee to another job within the company*	• Can the employee make a contribution elsewhere in the company? • Will a replacement requisition be cut if this person is transferred or terminated, or will I be left with no one to do the job? —Does the employee have the required intellectual and interpersonal capabilities? —Is the employee motivated to learn a new job? —Am I being realistic, or simply avoiding responsibility for termination by transferring a "problem" employee to another area?
3. *Start process of disciplinary action and termination*	• Have I given the employee every chance to succeed? —Has the employee had adequate resources to do the job? —Has the employee been sufficiently trained and oriented? —Has the employee been through counseling or coaching sessions? • Does the employee understand the expectations and job standards? • Has the employee made promises to improve and not kept these promises? • Is the individual's performance disrupting the team's performance or affecting business results?

✔ TAKE DISCIPLINARY ACTION

If you have tried your best as a manager to help an employee improve his or her performance and your efforts have not helped, you will need to initiate disciplinary action. Disciplinary action should be reserved for situations when improvement does not occur in a reasonable amount of time. In such cases, discipline should be spelled out in advance, and it should come as a corrective and logical consequence. No surprises or arbitrary actions like "lowering the boom" should occur. Even if discipline is used, action plans to improve performance should be developed. This section will help you carry out that action.

Definition

Disciplinary Action: A formal management system designed to get the employee to accept responsibility for his or her own behavior and agree to improve performance or face specific prescribed alternatives.

1. DOCUMENT EMPLOYEE'S PERFORMANCE

The manager needs to keep an informal file on each employee, recording dates and times of the counseling or coaching sessions. The manager's notes should include what was discussed, what was agreed upon and whether performance problems have improved, stayed the same or deteriorated. Specific and measurable performance objectives should be defined in any disciplinary action plan. Before terminating an employee for poor performance, the manager should have a minimum of six counseling sessions recorded over a minimum period of six weeks.

2. INVOLVE HUMAN RESOURCES OR PERSONNEL

Make sure you are working within your organization's policies when instituting a disciplinary action. Check with your Human Resources or Personnel Manager *before* you move into the "Required Steps in Disciplinary Action" shown in the next section.

3. GET YOUR MANAGER'S SUPPORT

Make sure your judgments and decisions are supported by *your* manager. It is wise to keep him or her informed during the disciplinary action process. It is also a good idea to solicit his or her advice and approval.

Required Steps in Disciplinary Action

Level 1: Verbal Warning

A verbal warning is a conversation between an employee and manager to correct a performance problem by formally bringing it to the attention of the employee. After meeting with the employee, the manager may wish to prepare a memo of the verbal warning for the files. If such a memo is prepared, a copy should be given to the employee. Verbal warnings are best given in private.

Level 2: Written Reminder

If the employee fails to make the desired performance changes following a verbal warning, a Level 2 action should be taken. A written reminder is documentation of a formal discussion between a manager and an employee regarding a performance problem. The discussion is followed by a letter written to the employee, which summarizes the conversation. A copy of this letter is generally sent to Human Resources and put in the employee's file.

Level 3: Termination Discussion

Manager informs the employee that he or she is terminated from the company, giving specific reasons that relate to the Level 2 written reminder. The manager, in conjunction with Human Resources, is responsible for all termination and severance arrangements.*

---

* For in-depth coverage of this subject, order *Rightful Termination: Avoiding Litigation*, by Ron Visconti and Richard Stiller, Menlo Park, CA: Crisp, 1994.

TERMINATION

In order to avoid a wrongful discharge suit against the company, a manager should follow the Required Disciplinary Action Steps listed previously. However, in the following situations, a manager may consider the immediate suspension of the employee. Check your company policy on these situations before taking action.

- Theft of company property

- Intentional damage to company property

- Hostile relationships with customers

- Criminal behavior

- Insubordination

- Any violence or threats of violence by an employee against the life, health, well-being, family or property of others, made while on the company premises, at company functions or in other circumstances, which may have an adverse impact on the company's ability to do business.

When Terminating a Potentially Violent Employee

Do Not

Conduct the discussion if you are the target of the employee's threats or obsessions. Find a Human Resources professional to conduct the session.

Negotiate over anything.

Argue with the employee about the company, management, etc.

Get into specifics about the past behavior.

Make threats.

Hurt the employee's self-esteem.

Discuss how the employee could have kept the job.

Use threatening body language.

Promise special severance arrangements.

Allow your own emotions to make you lose control.

TERMINATION (continued)

When Terminating a Potentially Violent Employee

Treat the individual with respect and dignity.

Try to stay calm. Rehearse ahead of time and write down what you will say.

Prepare for the worst realistic outcome—just in case. If the potential for violence is high, have internal security personnel nearby or even in the room.

State your understanding of the situation (bizarre behavior, threats, altercations, etc.), based on your investigation.

Keep the discussion short and general, focusing on company policy.

State, "We have no choice but to (suspend or terminate) you due to unacceptable behavior according to our company policies."

Let the person know that you think he or she will behave in a professional manner.

Describe the severance arrangements and logistics.

Emphasize the future—that you know he or she can be successful elsewhere.

Collect all company property—keys, access cards, etc. Make sure the termination is complete.

MY ACTION PLAN

It is essential that you act *now* to stay informed about prevention strategies. To develop your skills and retain your new knowledge on the subject of violence in the workplace, you need an action plan. To create a specific action plan, answer the following questions:

1. How can I assist my company in assembling a crisis management team?

_____

2. How can I increase my knowledge of professional resources to assist me?

_____

3. How can I help my company formulate a crisis management plan?

_____

4. How can I help my company establish a violence-prevention plan?

_____

5. What gaps do I have in my knowledge of employment laws?

_____

6. How can I more effectively screen out potentially violent employees?

_____

7. How can I do a better job of spotting potential problem employees?

_____

8. How can I be a more effective coach and counselor?

_____

9. How can I use positive strategies when suspending or terminating an employee?

_____

SECTION

III

Crisis Management

" In adversity, remember to keep an even mind. "

—Horace, 65–8 B.C

RECOGNIZE AND MOBILIZE

Workplace violence can begin with something as simple as an exchange of angry words, but it can lead to events as devastating as murder. Managers must be alert to disruptive behaviors that are repetitive. These should be considered critical incidents that require intervention. If they increase in intensity, they threaten the safety of employees and company property. At the very least they disrupt the normal operations of the business and may damage the public image of the company.

When a critical incident occurs, your crisis management team should be mobilized immediately, to determine what steps to take. *Never attempt to handle these situations single-handedly.* Rely on the trained internal and external support you have readied to provide the expertise you need.

> **Remember:** In a volatile situation or critical incident, your primary responsibility is the safety of your employees and yourself.

This section contains material to assist you once repetitive disruptive behavior has occurred, or actual threats have been made.

WHAT TO DO DURING A CRISIS

Following are guidelines you should follow for taking action once disruptive behavior has intensified, a threat has been made or a violent incident has occurred. Keep in mind that an emergency situation will most certainly require quicker decision making than these guidelines allow. Understanding and preparing for these steps will assist you in making good decisions FAST.

1. Take All Specific Threats Seriously

Though most threats are never carried out, it is critical that you pay heed to all threats. By examining the warning signs discussed earlier in this book and carefully evaluating perceived danger, you will have taken a major step toward intervention and toward protecting your company and its employees. Misjudgment at this stage may have serious consequences.

2. Pull Together Your Crisis Management Team

Immediately gather the members of your team. Hire or notify legal advisors to evaluate all potential legal ramifications and consequences to the business. Hire or notify assessment professionals to analyze the threats and potential future violence and recommend appropriate action. Decide with the members of your team when to communicate specific facts to employees and others affected by the crisis.

MORE STEPS TO TAKE DURING A CRITICAL INCIDENT . . .

3. Investigate and Interview

If time and safety allow, conduct an investigation of the allegations of violence, using internal and external resources where possible, before warning other employees. *Verify* the source of the allegations and *document* the following information:

- The exact statement made or action taken

- Circumstances under which the statement or action occurred

- Any knowledge the source has of the alleged perpetrator

- The relationship between the source and the alleged perpetrator

- Names of others who have witnessed the incident, who have personal knowledge of other threats or odd behavior by the same person, or who have detailed knowledge of the alleged perpetrator

Have one individual conduct all interviews if possible, and keep the information obtained during interviews confidential.

Assure the employee who reported the incident that he or she did the right thing in reporting it. Find out if he or she has any suggestions to minimize the risk of violence, especially if he or she knows the alleged perpetrator. Finally, advise the reporting employee of your conclusions and the steps you plan to take to control the situation.

4. Meet with the Threat Maker or Perpetrator

Determine who should be present during the meeting with the employee. If an unpredictable employee has been fired or laid off, have security personnel nearby. Get the alleged perpetrator's side of the story; listen to his or her concerns and pay attention to the issues involved. It is important, however, not to negotiate during disciplinary discussions, suspensions or terminations. Stand firm on your decisions.

Later in this section you'll find some suggestions for using and understanding nonverbal communication; this is an important element in meeting with a troubled person.

WHAT TO DO DURING A CRISIS
(continued)

5. Take Action

If the situation allows, consider suspending the employee pending a thorough investigation of the allegations. If you are convinced that the threat is genuine and danger is imminent, suspend the employee immediately. Take action to separate a violent employee from other employees and customers, to avoid negligent retention suits. Encourage the threat maker to resign if that will reduce tensions and avoid conflict and potential violence.

Remember that it is your legal responsibility to protect the rights of the threat maker, as well as other employees. Be careful not to respond hastily or improperly while you are assessing the risk of the situation.

Prohibit the employee from returning to the workplace until the investigation is complete; take away his or her keys, access cards, badges, and so forth. Consider extra security measures.

At this point, other decisions made by your crisis management team will need to be implemented.

6. Make Appropriate Efforts to Communicate with Others

Have a liaison ready to act as communicator with police, emergency teams and other external support personnel. Direct another person to contact families of potential victims. (Both of these people should be chosen by the crisis management team.)

Obtain temporary restraining orders against harassers, if necessary.

TEN PITFALLS TO AVOID DURING A CRITICAL INCIDENT

Make sure you and the members of your crisis management team do not make any of the following errors in handling a critical incident:

1. Discounting or ignoring ominous threats.

2. Allowing the supervisor who is a possible victim to conduct the investigation of or interview with the alleged perpetrator.

3. Failing to have company or outside security personnel nearby when the threat of violence appears to be genuine and you are conducting disciplinary discussions with the employee.

4. Avoiding suspension of the perpetrator pending the conclusion of the investigation, because you are afraid of the consequences. (The problem will most likely get worse, not better.)

5. Using confrontational behavior, such as threatening a criminal investigation, raising your voice or using intimidating body language.

6. Disregarding crisis procedures outlined by the crisis management team.

7. Neglecting communication with employees who need to know of possible threats or pending danger, after the threat has been determined to be real.

8. When seeking a restraining order, failing to warn potential victims of possible violence, so they can take extra precautions.

9. Acting on impulse and terminating an employee on the spot, without conducting an investigation or following the key steps of disciplinary action.

10. Being manipulated by the perpetrator into allowing extra latitude, permitting lower standards or accepting inappropriate behavior.

TIPS ON NONVERBAL COMMUNICATION

Pay attention to the nonverbal communication that you express toward the threat maker or violent individual and that he or she exhibits toward you. Communication experts point out that 10 to 15 percent of the message we deliver to another person is the verbal element; 85 to 90 percent of the message is *nonverbal.* Remember these tips:

► Give the potentially violent person enough physical space. Although this varies by culture, in the U.S., two to four feet away is considered an adequate distance.

► Avoid glaring or staring, which may be perceived as a challenge.

► Stay conscious of how you are delivering your words. Keep the volume low, and speak slowly.

► Listen carefully. Use empathetic listening; don't be judgmental. Use silence as a calming tool, and paraphrase to clarify what you are hearing.

► Observe the individual's body language. Use caution if the person exhibits one or more of the following:

- red face
- sweating
- pacing
- trembling or shaking
- crossed arms and legs

- clenched jaws or fists
- exaggerated gestures
- shallow, rapid breathing
- scowling or sneering
- glaring or avoiding eye contact

► Remain as calm as possible.

HELPING EMPLOYEES GET THROUGH THE TRAUMA

One need not be the direct recipient of violence to be a victim. Employees who witness acts of violence against others—even those who hear about the incident later—can experience the same shock, anger, grief and vulnerability that more "direct" victims feel. All victims need to receive the company's support.

Neglecting victim support can damage a company in various ways. Employees are likely to be substantially less productive in the aftermath of trauma, and if this stage is not handled properly, the company's ability to function may suffer. The company may also incur legal liability for failing to provide adequate response and services to employee victims. In one study on the after-effects of violence, *94 percent of victims of emotional trauma in the workplace who received no treatment until 6 to 36 months after the incident sued their employers.*

Whether they choose litigation or not, employees with unresolved rage and grief may channel these feelings toward the company, creating significant damage to corporate loyalty.

One of the most important steps you as a manager can take after a critical incident is to provide immediate counseling and trauma therapy for your employees. Obtain the services of professionals who can help the group resolve powerful negative feelings in the wake of trauma. Companies *must not* neglect the human side of crisis. The effects will not go away by themselves.

TALKING WITH A POTENTIAL VICTIM

► Talk to the potential victim *as soon as possible* after the danger has been identified. Inform the individual of the possible range of behaviors the perpetrator might display, and suggest options for preventing a crisis.

► Document ahead of time what you will tell the potential victim (it may be needed later in litigation).

► Document the threat itself, and get statements from others who have heard or observed the perpetrator.

► Offer the potential victim the opportunity for security protection.

► Ask the potential victim what he or she needs from you to increase his or her comfort level.

FACTS YOU SHOULD KNOW ABOUT TRAUMA

The following facts and statistics about the after-effects of violence will help you understand the major impact violence has on people's lives.

- One hundred percent of crime victims report major changes afterward in their lives and families.

- Traumatized employees are likely to be substantially less productive in the aftermath of trauma.

- Victims of crimes are ten times more likely to become severely depressed than nonvictims.

- About 200,000 new cases of post-traumatic stress disorder occur each year, with related costs of approximately $100 billion annually.

- Victims of workplace violence go through predictable phases in the recovery process.

- The severity of the response to witnessing or experiencing violence is affected by the length of the incident and how much warning there was prior to the incident.

- After a critical incident, most victims feel substantial vulnerability and that "nowhere is safe."

- Employees who have suffered many losses and do not have a strong support system may experience a difficult recovery process.

- How a company acknowledges the grieving process and provides support can make a big difference in how quickly employees get back to work.

EMPLOYEE TRAUMA CHECKLIST

Employees who are victims of workplace violence have reactions quite similar to other victims of violence and crime. In the following list, check the responses that you believe occur.

☐ Mood swings

☐ Alcohol and drug abuse

☐ Sleep disorders

☐ Eating disorders

☐ Psychosomatic disorders (stomach pain, headaches, etc.)

☐ Panic or anxiety attacks

☐ Family tension and stress

☐ Lack of ability to concentrate

☐ Nonspecific fears

☐ Low morale and productivity

☐ Feelings of helplessness

☐ Feelings of isolation and loneliness

☐ Anger and rage

☐ Increased sense of vulnerability

☐ Flashbacks of the event

All of the above reactions are reported by victims of workplace violence.

WHAT TO DO AFTER A CRITICAL INCIDENT

To lessen the effects of the crisis and promote the beginning of the healing process:

Address Your Employees' Reactions

Provide individual and group support sessions, including help for victims' families. Strongly encourage those who witnessed the incident to talk, and help them explore their thoughts and reactions. Encourage voluntary, not mandatory, participation at support sessions.

Make every attempt to validate employees' feelings and let them know they are entitled to their feelings. Encourage employees to visit the site of the incident, as a way of working through the grieving process.

Identify the high-risk individuals as soon as possible. Let them know the company cares about them; offer support and counseling, and flexible job conditions if possible. Consider offering 24-hour telephone counseling to those affected.

Address Your Managers' Concerns

Conduct a special workshop for managers on how they can effectively supervise employees who are having stress reactions, and gradually get them back to productive work.

If you are a senior manager, assess the ability of your other managers to cope with work demands. If necessary, give time off and/or temporarily suspend certain operations of the business to allow people time to grieve and adjust.

Gather Professional Support

Employ the appropriate outside experts in handling trauma. These may include psychologists, counselors, employee assistance programs and assessment professionals. If there are continued threats, work closely with police and security consultants.

Arrange for Proper Communication

Give employees verbal and written information about what happened. Acknowledge their pain and explain the company's plan for helping everyone through the transition.

Make sure your crisis management team has chosen an experienced spokesperson to manage communication with the media. Give the press the most honest, complete information you can about the incident, while protecting the company's and employees' legal rights and privacy.

Communicate with shareholders and others with interest in the firm, providing information about the incident and how the company will deal with it. Throughout the recovery process, make it a goal to maintain the goodwill of your clients and the community in general. Assure customers that they are not being forgotten, and ask for their patience.

Reassess and Improve Preventive Measures

Working with your crisis management team, assess how the overall crisis was handled. Review what worked and what didn't, and determine what procedures need to be refined. Evaluate the current security provisions for company buildings and grounds.

Continue to provide ongoing training for managers on assessing potential violence and detecting warning signs. Carry forward the positive management strategies you already have in place, and improve them if need be.

Work toward being even better prepared for possible future incidents.

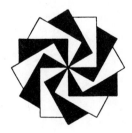 

AFTER A CRITICAL INCIDENT: DON'TS AND DOS

The following list of don'ts and dos can serve as a guideline for managers to follow with employees after a critical incident. By being aware of the impact of the violence and making adjustments for the emotional aftermath, managers can help prepare the way to getting the workplace restored and ready to get back to full productivity.

(DO NOT)

- Assume that employees will return immediately to "business as usual"

- Believe that employees will be "rational" about the critical incident

- Expect the same level of employee performance as before the incident

- Feel guilty and that you could or should have done something to stop the incident

- Deny your own feelings about the incident

(DO)

- Designate personnel to be responsible for logistics (transportation for employees, meeting payroll, etc.)

- Appoint one particular spokesperson to handle press releases and media contact

- Hire a clean-up crew to restore the work environment

- Have a plan for handling normal business responsibilities, such as phone calls, orders, deliveries, and so on

- Be available to listen to employees' concerns

SECTION

IV

Case Studies

"Let us not forget that man can never get away from himself."

—Goethe

TEST YOUR KNOWLEDGE

In most organizations a manager must quickly render a judgment of violence potential based on limited information. In the following case studies, you can be the judge using this limited information.

Note: Any similarities between these case studies and actual situations is strictly coincidental and not the intention of the author.

Options for Action

In each of the following case studies, choose one or more of the options below. You can write in more options if you like. After you complete your analysis and choose the best options, see how close your answers match those listed at the bottom of each case study.

1. Conduct an investigation of the allegations of violence.

2. Document the who, what, when, where, why and how of the critical incident.

3. Defuse the immediate crisis by using active listening techniques and setting limits.

4. Hire outside legal expertise to advise you.

5. Consult assessment professionals to analyze the threats and the employee, and to make recommendations.

6. Arrange comprehensive outplacement services.

7. Conduct performance coaching and/or counseling.

8. Suspend the employee until an investigation is completed.

9. Terminate the employee immediately due to policy violation.

10. Implement the steps of disciplinary action: verbal warnings, written warnings, etc.

11. Obtain a restraining order to protect yourself and/or the threatened employee, and your families.

TEST YOUR KNOWLEDGE (continued)

12. Report the incident to the crisis management team if one exists. If one does not, report the incident to senior management *and* Human Resources.

13. Contact Human Resources about company policies on sexual harassment.

14. Get the alleged perpetrator's side of the story, listen to his or her concerns and pay attention to the issues involved.

15. Inform the potential victim of the problem and the possible range of behaviors the perpetrator might display. Suggest options for preventing a crisis.

16. Offer the potential victim security protection.

17. Call police *now*.

18. Encourage the employee to use employee assistance programs for professional counseling.

19. Provide individual and group grief counseling to all employees.

20. Gather your crisis management team to deal with the media, customers, victims and their families.

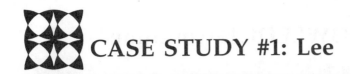

CASE STUDY #1: Lee

Sam has been a worker in a semiconductor manufacturing firm for five years and has been frequently transferred throughout the company due to interpersonal difficulties. During the six months Lee has been supervising Sam, she has observed that Sam has had a tough time dealing with change, has been unable to shift his priorities when business conditions require it, and has become defensive when given constructive feedback.

One day Lee attends a manager's meeting, where she overhears two women, Sam's previous managers, discussing his behavior. Both say he has been very hostile to them, calling them obscene names when they requested that he shift priorities. They also say he has been verbally abusive to peers, as well, particularly to females.

Lee decides it is time to do something about the situation and calls Sam to set up an appointment. She decides to coach Sam about his relationship with peers and managers. As soon as the session with Sam begins, Lee attempts to get Sam to see the consequences of his behavior. He stands up and says, "You women are all alike and think you can push me around. If you don't stop pushing me, I'm going to kill you." Lee is aghast and does not know what to say or do next.

What do you think should happen?

Case Study #1 Review

_____

_____

_____

_____

_____

_____

Options 2, 3 5, 8, 12

TEST YOUR KNOWLEDGE (continued)

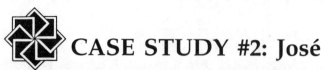 CASE STUDY #2: José

Tom has been a postal clerk for six years, and José has been his manager for two of those years. Tom has been a good employee until two months ago, when he became irritable and agitated and developed an attraction for another employee, Sally. Sally has been quite clear with Tom that she is not interested in pursuing a relationship with him.

Tom does not seem to hear Sally and continues to pursue her on and off the job, to her dismay. He has even followed her home from work to get her address. Except for this harassment of Sally, Tom's performance meets job expectations.

Sally has come to José, also her manager, to discuss her feelings and concerns. When Sally arrived at work early this morning, Tom was waiting in her office with flowers and tickets to a concert. He told her that if she didn't go with him, he would make sure "she would suffer."

What should José do?

Case Study #2 Review

_____
_____
_____
_____
_____
_____

Options 2, 5, 12, 13, 14, 15, 18

CASE STUDY #3: Marsha

Marsha, a first-time supervisor in a manufacturing company, is worried about Van, a 25-year-old immigrant who has been with the company for six months. Marsha has told Van that he will be laid off in a month due to a reduction in force. Van has told Marsha that his job is his whole life and he will kill himself if he loses it. Marsha feels terrible about the situation, as she knows he has few marketable skills and no support system in the United States.

What should Marsha do?

Case Study #3 Review

_____
_____
_____
_____
_____
_____

MORE CASE STUDIES AHEAD . . .

TEST YOUR KNOWELDGE (continued)

 ## CASE STUDY #4: Tony

Tony, a project manager in a nuclear power plant, has been supervising a team of quality control employees for the last two years. Work demands have increased lately due to budget cuts, reductions in force and demands for greater efficiency.

Tony is growing concerned about Joe, one of his team members, who seems to be getting more and more volatile. Joe's wife left him a month ago for another man in the company, Paul. Tony has listened to Joe's frustrations, but instead of diminishing over time, Joe's hostility is escalating. Over lunch today, Joe told Tony that he wants to "blow Paul away, along with my wife." And Tony happens to know that Joe has access to guns, because the two of them go duck hunting every fall.

Tony doesn't want to overreact or get involved, but what should he do?

Case Study #4 Review

_____

_____

_____

_____

_____

_____

CASE STUDY #5: Kyle

Kyle, a marketing manager in a high-tech company, has had a tough time with his employee, Mark, a computer salesman. Over the last year Kyle has coached and counseled Mark several times on how to deal with difficult customers. Mark seems to have a short fuse and gets hostile and defensive during these coaching sessions, blaming the difficulties on "those stupid customers." He does not see how he could change his behavior to be more successful. The company has lost two key accounts because Mark did not build effective relationships with the clients, and Kyle is at the end of his rope. He has put Mark on a written disciplinary plan during their last session.

As Kyle walks by Mark's office one day, he overhears Mark saying on the phone, "If they try to fire me, I'm going to destroy all the computers in the office and make them regret the day they ever messed with me." Kyle found out just last week from a friend at a professional network that Mark was fired from his last job due to a violent altercation with a customer.

What do you think Kyle should do?

Case Study #5 Review

_____

_____

_____

_____

_____

_____

Options 2, 5, 9, 12

TEST YOUR KNOWLEDGE (continued)

CASE STUDY #6: Dale

Dale is manager of an administrative group in a financial services institution. Karen, a clerical worker, reports to Dale. Karen has been repeatedly threatened by her ex-husband, Jim, who has said he will kill her if he sees her with another man. Jim suspects, irrationally, that Karen is having an affair with Dale and has made threatening phone calls to Dale at work and at home. Jim has a history of violent behavior and drug abuse, and he physically abused Karen badly when they were married. As her manager, Dale has tried to support Karen by referring her to employee assistance programs and legal advisors to get a restraining order against her ex-husband.

Dale has just returned home after a long, hard day. As he opens his garage, he sees Jim's car pull up in front of the house.

If you were Dale, what would you do?

Case Study #6 Review

_____

_____

_____

_____

_____

_____

Options 5, 11, 15, 16, 17

CASE STUDY #7: X Corporation

Arthur, a laid-off employee who has filed numerous grievance complaints against his supervisors at X Corporation, a defense contractor, arrived one day at his former workplace with a rifle and shotgun. He killed the vice-president and general manager of the plant and the regional sales manager. He then killed himself in front of several employees.

What action should X Corporation take after this critical incident?

Case Study #7 Review

_____
_____
_____
_____
_____
_____

CASE STUDIES 7–10 AHEAD . . .

Options 19, 20

TEST YOUR KNOWLEDGE (continued)

 CASE STUDY #8: Maria

Maria, a Human Resources vice-president in a computer company, knows she has some tough times ahead. She has been told to assist in a reduction in force; 500 company employees will be released by the end of the month. She has also been told that she must cut 10 people from her remaining staff.

She is most worried about Mike, a 58-year-old HR Representative with a history of performance problems. Mike's previous managers failed to document his substandard performance; nor did they hold Mike accountable for his failures. So the problem has fallen to Maria, who has been coaching and counseling him for one year but with no improvement.

Maria knows that Mike has a drinking problem and that he has become bitter toward the company and management in general. His clients complain about his behavior. In fact, one of his clients revealed this morning that Mike said if he got laid off, he was going to seek revenge on "those big-shot managers at the top."

What can Maria do to prevent this situation from escalating?

Case Study #8 Review

_____

_____

_____

_____

_____

_____

Options 2, 10, 12

CASE STUDY #9: Mohammed

Mohammed, a middle manager in a software company, is concerned about Melinda, one of the software engineers. She is very competent, with a great career ahead of her. Unfortunately, she has had serious psychological problems, and Mohammed knows she was hospitalized four years ago with a manic-depressive disorder, which was stabilized with medication.

Recently, he has noted significant changes in Melinda's behavior. She insists that other employees are talking about her, that work standards are impossible to reach, and that she is being singled out for more and more work. Mohammed has also noticed that she seems agitated and has an inflated sense of her own importance. When he has tried talking with her, she gets very defensive. During their last counseling session, she admitted she had stopped taking her medication. Then she said, "The president has been following me, and I know you are trying to get me fired."

How can Mohammed address this problem?

Case Study #9 Review

_____

_____

_____

_____

_____

TEST YOUR KNOWLEDGE (continued)

 ## CASE STUDY #10: Sandy

Sandy, a director of customer services at a bank, is growing increasingly concerned about her boss, Jerome, a vice-president who has been with the bank for 10 years. Sandy knows Jerome is under a great deal of pressure; she has heard through the grapevine that he is on a performance improvement program. He recently called a meeting with his team to get feedback that he could use to improve. When members started to give him constructive advice, however, he blew up and said, "We all know who does the work around here. I think you all want to see me fail. You're all out to get me."

Sandy was flabbergasted. At the end of the day, she stopped by Jerome's office to say goodnight, and he asked her to sit down and talk. He confided that he knew he was going to be fired and said he would not take it "lying down." He stated that he planned to "take a few people down" with him when he went.

What should Sandy do?

Case Study #10 Review

_____
_____
_____
_____
_____
_____

Options 2, 5, 12, 18

SECTION

V

Resource
Appendix

KNOW YOUR RESOURCES

The resources listed in this section are representative of the many available throughout North America. Please note that this is *not* an exhaustive list.

Employee Assistance Programs

Institute for Human Resources
Founded in 1981, the Institute for Human Resources (IHR) is a national/international provider of employee assistance services.
Corporate Headquarters
P.O. Box 1373, Mail Route 6320
Minneapolis, MN 55440
612-945-6620

250 North Sunnyslope Road, Suite 300
Brookfield, WI 53005
414-785-8118

CONCERN Employee Assistance Program
CONCERN offers education, counseling and trauma services.
2635 North First Street, Suite 223
San Jose, CA 95134
Phone: 408-432-0616
Fax: 408-432-0526

Assessment Professionals

Brian Lawton & David Brewer
One Sansome Street, Suite 2100
San Francisco, CA 94104
415-951-4744

National Assessment Services
(*Chris Hatcher*)
220 Montgomery Street, Suite 3308
San Francisco, CA 94104
415-388-0665

Work Trauma Services
(*Stephen White*)
110 Sutter Street, Suite 710
San Francisco, CA 94104
415-398-3966

KNOW YOUR RESOURCES (continued)

Michael M. Zanoni, Ph.D.
Investigator and Forensic Consultant
P.O. Box 369
San Carlos, CA 94070
415-349-8822

Legal Assistance

Holtzmann, Wise & Shepard
Philip Hyde
3030 Hansen Way, Suite 100
Palo Alto, CA 94304
415-856-1200

Schachter, Kristoff, Orenstein and Berkowitz
505 Montgomery Street, 14th Floor
San Francisco, CA 94111-2585
415-391-3333

Jack Early
19100 Van Karman, 8th Floor
Irvine, CA 92715
714-476-8900

Littler, Mendelson, Fastiff, Tichy and Mathiason
650 California Street
San Francisco, CA 94108
415-433-1940

Other Resources

For assistance in security matters, you can consult

John O'Laughlin
Security Consultant on Internal Corporate Security
Sun Microsystems, Inc.
901 San Antonio Road, Mail Stop PALI-407
Palo Alto, CA 94043
415–336-2217

National Crisis Prevention Institute, Inc.
The National Crisis Prevention Institute is an international training organization specializing in the safe management of assaultive and disruptive behavior.
3315 K, North 124th Street
Brookfield, WI 53005
414-783-5787
1-800-558-8976

National Trauma Services
National Trauma Services consults with business and professional groups regarding the prevention of and response to violence in the workplace.
3554 Front Street
San Diego, CA 92103
619-296-2811
1-800-398-2811

The International Critical Incident Stress Foundation, Inc.
The International Critical Incident Stress Foundation has a worldwide leadership role in developing and disseminating crisis intervention and stress education and recovery programs to those affected by work-related stress, disasters and other traumatic events.
5018 Dorsey Hall Drive, Suite 104
Elliot City, MD 21042
410-730-4311
410-313-CISD (emergency)

Institute for Crisis Management
The Institute for Crisis Management is a research organization focused on preventing and controlling business crises.
710 West Main Street, Suite 200
Louisville, KY 40202
502-584-0402

Crisis Management International, Inc. (CMI)
CMI is one of the largest, most experienced crisis management teams in the United States dealing with the human side of crises. CMI manages traumatic events in the workplace and provides traumatic stress debriefing and other interventions for organizations and employees after tragedies occur. CMI also helps companies develop crisis readiness plans, including management of traumatic stress in employees.
Eight Piedmont Center, Suite 420
Atlanta, GA 30305
404-841-3400

KNOW YOUR RESOURCES (continued)

Preemployment Testing

London House/Science Research Associates
London House specializes in preemployment integrity and safety tests, customized tests and legal issues in testing including the preemployment tests listed below.

Personnel Selection Inventory (PSI™)

- Dependability/Integrity
- Drug Avoidance
- Nonviolent Tendencies

London House
9701 West Higgins Road
Rosemont, IL 60018
1-800-221-8378
1-708-292-1900 in Illinois

BIBLIOGRAPHY

Bensimon, H. "Violence in the Workplace." *Info Line,* July 1993.

Fink, S. *Crisis Management: Planning for the Inevitable.* New York, NY: American Management Association, 1986.

Forward, S. *Obsessive Love.* New York: Bantam Books, 1991.

Franklin, F. "Over the Edge: Managing Violent Episodes." *Security Management Journal,* 1991.

Hatcher, C., and S. G. White. "Violence and Trauma Response." *Occupational Medicine: State of the Art Reviews,* vol. 3, no. 4, October–December 1988.

Hewitt, J., and T. Misner. "Female Workplace Homicides: An Integrative Research Review." *AAOHN Journal,* vol. 40, no. 5, May 1992.

Jenkins, E., L. Layne, and S. Kisner. "Homicide in the Workplace: The U.S. Experience 1980–1988." *AAOHN Journal,* vol. 40, no. 5, May 1992.

Kuzmits, F. "Workplace Homicide: Prediction or Prevention." *SAM Advanced Management Journal,* Spring 1992.

O'Boyle, T. "Disgruntled Workers Intent on Revenge Increasingly Harm Colleagues and Bosses." *The Wall Street Journal,* September 15, 1992.

Sauter, S., L. Murphy, and Hurrell. "Prevention of Work-Related Psychological Disorders." *American Psychologist,* vol. 45, no. 10, October 1990.

Silberman, C. *Criminal Violence, Criminal Justice.* New York: Random House, 1978.

Stuart, P. "Murder on the Job." *Personnel Journal,* February 1992.

Zanoni, M. "Empathy for Vengeance." *The Bulletin of the Institute of Criminology and Forensic Sciences,* October 1992.

NOTES

NOTES

NOTES

NOTES

NOTES

NOTES

NOTES

Now Available From

CRiSP Learning

Books•Videos•CD-ROMs•Computer-Based Training Products

Subject Areas Include:

Management
Human Resources
Communication Skills
Personal Development
Marketing/Sales
Organizational Development
Customer Service/Quality
Computer Skills
Small Business and Entrepreneurship
Adult Literacy and Learning
Life Planning and Retirement

CRISP WORLDWIDE DISTRIBUTION

English language books are distributed worldwide. Major international distributors include:

ASIA/PACIFIC

Australia/New Zealand: In Learning, PO Box 1051, Springwood QLD, Brisbane, Australia 4127   Tel: 61-7-3-841-2286, Facsimile: 61-7-3-841-1580 ATTN: Messrs. Richard/Robert Gordon

Hong Kong/Mainland China: Crisp Learning Solutions, 18/F Honest Motors Building 9-11 Leighton Road, Causeway Bay, Hong Kong   Tel: 852-2915-7119, Facsimile: 852-2865-2815 ATTN: Ms. Grace Lee

Indonesia: Pt Lutan Edukasi, Citra Graha, 7th Floor, Suite 701A, Jl. Jend. Gato Subroto Kav. 35-36, Jakarta 12950 Indonesia Tel: 62-21-527-9060/527-9061 Facsimile: 62-21-527-9062 ATTN: Mr. Suwardi Luis

Japan: Phoenix Associates, Believe Mita Bldg., 8th Floor 3-43-16 Shiba, Minato-ku, Tokyo 105-0014, Japan   Tel: 81-3-5427-6231, Facsimile: 81-3-5427-6232 ATTN: Mr. Peter Owans

Malaysia, Philippines, Singapore: Epsys Pte Ltd., 540 Sims Avenue #04-01, Sims Avenue Centre, 387603, Singapore   Tel: 65-747-1964, Facsimile: 65-747-0162 ATTN: Mr. Jack Chin

CANADA

Crisp Learning Canada, 60 Briarwood Avenue, Mississauga, ON L5G 3N6 Canada Tel: 905-274-5678, Facsimile: 905-278-2801 ATTN: Mr. Steve Connolly

EUROPEAN UNION

England: Flex Learning Media, Ltd., 9-15 Hitchin Street, Baldock, Hertfordshire, SG7 6AL, England Tel: 44-1-46-289-6000, Facsimile: 44-1-46-289-2417   ATTN: Mr. David Willetts

INDIA

Multi-Media HRD, Pvt. Ltd., National House, Floor 1, 6 Tulloch Road, Appolo Bunder, Bombay, India 400-039 Tel: 91-22-204-2281, Facsimile: 91-22-283-6478 ATTN: Messrs. Ajay Aggarwal/ C.L. Aggarwal

SOUTH AMERICA

Mexico: Grupo Editorial Iberoamerica, Nebraska 199, Col. Napoles, 03810 Mexico, D.F. Tel: 525-523-0994, Facsimile: 525-543-1173   ATTN: Señor Nicholas Grepe

SOUTH AFRICA

Corporate: Learning Resources, PO Box 2806, Parklands, Johannesburg 2121, South Africa, Tel: 27-21-531-2923, Facsimile: 27-21-531-2944 ATTN: Mr. Ricky Robinson

MIDDLE EAST

Edutech Middle East, L.L.C., PO Box 52334, Dubai U.A.E. Tel: 971-4-359-1222, Facsimile: 971-4-359-6500   ATTN: Mr. A.S.F. Karim